FOLLOWING THE LAMB
...wherever He goes

Richard George

short course

resources@thewayofthespirit.com
www.thewayofthespirit.com

Published in Great Britain in 2009
by The Way of the Spirit, Norfolk, UK

2nd Edition published in 2012
3rd Edition published in 2015
4th Edition published in 2016

Copyright © 2012 Richard George

All rights reserved. No part of this publication may be reproduced, stored in a retrieval system, or transmitted, in any form or by any means, electronic, mechanical, photocopying, recording or otherwise, without the permission, in writing, of the publisher.

ISBN 978-1-9085-2826-1

Scripture taken from the
HOLY BIBLE, NEW INTERNATIONAL VERSION.
Copyright © 1973, 1978, 1984 by the International Bible Society. Used by permission of Hodder and Stoughton Limited.

Bible Reading Course

The purpose of this booklet and the recorded teaching that goes with it is partly to give you some impression of how The Way of the Spirit Bible Reading Course works. It is not, however, just an excerpt or collection of excerpts from the fuller course, but a properly integrated short course in its own right, and as such is somewhat different in presentation.

- The full course takes you systematically through the whole Bible, chapter by chapter, with the help of a textbook; here you have only a little booklet giving a brief survey of a Bible theme.

- The full course has more comprehensive worksheets.

- The course recordings offer more systematic teaching arranged in twenty-minute parts.

Nevertheless, by using these materials you should capture the flavour of the full course quite well. The purpose of The Way of the Spirit is to teach about the aliveness of the Bible and the power of the Spirit revealed in its pages, to help you understand what the Bible is all about, what the way of God's Spirit is in it, and how to enter more fully into the richness of life men of Bible-times enjoyed. You should find all these aims met in some measure as you use **Following the Lamb**.

If after completing this short study you wish to proceed to the fuller course, please e-mail us at resources@thewayofthespirit.com or visit our web site at www.thewayofthespirit.com

May God bless you richly as you study his Word.

How to Use This Booklet

It is arranged in two parts:

- The first (pages 1-46) introduces the study.
- The second (pages 47-59) is a five-part reading guide.

Recorded teaching to accompany the booklet is also available.[1]

You can use this booklet in several different ways:

- By itself with your Bible.
- Along with the recording and your Bible.
- By studying in a group.

Whichever method you choose, learn to listen for what the Holy Spirit has to tell you—about your beliefs, attitudes and life-style. Ask yourself what lessons you should be learning from your readings, so that you can apply them to your own understanding and life as a Christian.

Part Two, the reading guide, has introductory notes on page 47 with further suggestions about how to use it. Each part of this section has questions that will help you determine what you have learned and

---

[1] You can listen to or download the teaching free of charge from our website at www.thewayofthespirit.com/audio.

encourage you to apply that in practical living. The notes have been prepared in such a way that you can use them privately or in a group. Experience has shown that group study is much more fruitful.

If you use the recorded teaching, you may find it best to listen to them before you start your readings. If you do this, you should also listen to them again afterwards. Not all the answers to the questions will be found in the booklet—this is intentional!

If you use this booklet in a group you will need to listen to the recording in your meeting. Then discuss your answers to the questions, share your insights and encourage one another to grow in the Lord. Remember to allow time for prayer and fellowship as well.

Preface to 1st Edition

Paul says *the man without the Spirit does not accept the things that come from the Spirit of God, for they are foolishness to him, and he cannot understand them, because they are spiritually discerned.*[2] I once prayed a life changing prayer! I said, in a moment of some rashness though with utmost seriousness, *Lord make me a spiritual man!* There may have been many who, maybe in exasperation, have prayed that prayer for me, and there are no doubt still many more longing for the day when that prayer might be fully answered! It was a prayer that has led me through some times that I would never have chosen for myself.

The truth is that to walk as a spiritual person, with spiritual understanding, is a different thing from walking in worldly wisdom. I don't mean spiritual-*sounding*, you know, those who make everything sound so spiritual and give the impression of being from another planet, nor do I mean those that are so ethically correct in the way they live their lives that everyone around them is made to feel as though they've hardly begun to follow Christ. But rather to live one's life as one who believes what God says is truer than whatever we may perceive with our natural senses - to live determined to hear what God

---

[2] 1 Corinthians 2.14

is saying and to walk in obedience to it, unto God and for his glory alone. Someone walking this way seeks to find out God's answer at every twist and turn, as they know it is only his answer—his way—that will lead to true life. They may get allured from time to time by things in the world but time and time again will return to seeking first the Kingdom and his righteousness, knowing that if they do then all other things will be added unto them—even if sometimes those things seem far away and even the other side of eternity!

Perhaps one of the biggest challenges in the church is for us to walk as spiritual men and women. There is so much around that can distract us in this endeavour, things looking spiritual enough but actually which more reflect the individualistic, material and consumerist society we live in, there to tempt us away from the cost of true discipleship.

Sometimes it's not easy to discern what's what as we have for so long been conditioned that being 'spiritual' looks a certain way! It may just mean sometimes doing the thing that looks least spiritual, for it is not about dualistic ways of separating things into sacred or secular but about truly walking in relationship with God, fearing him first and him alone. Any other way at best offers temporary solutions; his is the only way that leads to eternal life.

If things are not always as they seem, where is the roadmap for discovering the right way? Alas there isn't one—all we have is a relationship with Jesus in whom we live and move and have our being. Even his word, the Bible, isn't enough—it needs the breath of his Spirit on it, and we only learn to really hear *that* out of a living and dynamic relationship with him: one of obedience and Lordship. No keys, steps, formulas or methods; just relationship.

Following Jesus then is the only way to become 'spiritual'—we throw our anchor into eternity and see where it takes us. Once we have set our faces like flint to following him then we face every consequence with him, and cry out to him and him alone. He leads, and grows, and changes us as we follow him. It's what John McKay, I think, used to call the *prophetic call*— the famous highway of holiness. Sadly many opt for another, lesser, form of discipleship, where it's much safer: they stay where the water rarely gets rough and where there's a secure harbour wall.

So I guess this course is something to do with just that: following the Lamb wherever he goes.

Richard George - July 2009

Preface to 4th Edition

In this edition I have taken the opportunity to rework substantial portions of the text in order to bring some clarification, particularly in the middle section. Other parts remain unchanged, and the essence of the study is also unaltered.

Richard George - February 2016

FOLLOWING THE LAMB
...wherever He goes

1.

FOLLOWING THE LAMB PART ONE

Introduction

What happens when we follow Jesus? Storms and testing.

They were on their way up to Jerusalem with Jesus leading the way, and the disciples were astonished, while those who followed were afraid.[3]

A bedraggled group moves awkwardly along the roadway. They are subdued and apprehensive, uncertain of what lies ahead and talking quietly amongst themselves. Jesus, also thoughtful and somewhat preoccupied, nevertheless seems quite sure where he's going, self-assured and resolute in every stride as he leads the way.

Why leave Galilee? It had been such an exciting couple of years or so; Jesus had collected a great

---

[3] Mark 10.32

FOLLOWING THE LAMB
...wherever He goes

following and it really felt as if the Messiah had finally arrived. There had been so much action, it had been like a whirlwind. There had been authentic miracles and genuine scenes of joy and restoration in even the most broken lives. So where are they going now? They were headed for Jerusalem, but what could they hope to achieve there, amongst the temple officials, and with so many of the occupying Roman army present? Even their religious leaders didn't seem to want Jesus around.

Nevertheless they continued to follow, Jesus tenaciously setting the pace out in front, those accompanying him puzzled, and not a little afraid.

It's often like this following Jesus. It's certainly not like some evangelists say—you know, at the beginning. Some of them promise you an end to all your problems, an easy ride, 'Jesus your friend comes and takes away all your problems.' (He ultimately does of course, but not always quite in the way we'd like!)

It can be more like that time in Galilee when the disciples followed Jesus and headed straight into a storm. He called them to follow, climbed into a boat, and his disciples duly did. Then without warning a furious storm came up on the lake. What happens when we follow Jesus? Storms and testing! The disciples panicked and Jesus slept.

You of little faith, why are you so afraid? Jesus asked them. Why indeed? Why do we lack faith? Even after

FOLLOWING THE LAMB
...wherever He goes

years of following him we can find ourselves reacting in fear and sheer unadulterated unbelief. Lord help us— and he does, by allowing more storms until we finally begin to really get hold of the reality of his fatherhood, sovereignty and presence with us. (Worse, we may never step out and follow where he leads, choosing instead to stay on land where it's safe and dry. We're 'saved' but we never bear the fruit God intends us to—instead we duck the challenges designed to make us into the instruments for his glory).

Clearly, following Jesus isn't about walking cocooned from the world; it's not about being shielded from discomfort, squalls or even hurricanes. When we step out and follow him though, we learn to weather the storms, after we've survived a few they don't seem quite as big as they used to. Like Jesus we can even learn to stay in the right place, eventually perhaps even sleeping right through them.

Before they even got as far as stepping into the boat he hints at the cost of following him: [4] One of them then wants to go to his father's funeral and Jesus tells him let the dead bury their own dead. What on the face of it appears to be a rather unsympathetic reply mimics Elijah's impatience with Elisha, who had similarly wanted to wrap up his affairs at home before becoming his disciple. *What have I done to you?* Elijah cried out. Deep calls to deep and once

---

[4] Matthew 8.20

FOLLOWING THE LAMB
...wherever He goes

called it is hard to tolerate attitudes that don't somehow match the zeal the man of God carries.[5]

Jesus and Elijah each express the prophetic call of God which, when it arrives, touches us deeply and changes us forever. No cost seems too great to follow the call and we find it hard to comprehend anyone else's failure to match our fervour. Of course to start with—in us if not in Jesus (we don't ever read of Elijah's early days)—that fervour can be shrouded in immaturity and early enthusiasm. Yet God has put it there despite our not yet being ready, and after undergoing much testing promises we will come forth as gold.

Following Jesus means walking into and through the testing. That's why we're to follow him rather than our own self-protective or 'religious' instincts. When we really start to follow him wherever he goes life starts getting interesting: we have to change.

That's what Jesus meant when he counselled us to *buy from me only gold refined in the fire,*[6] for it is only that which has been tested which counts. What he puts in us is no use to others until it has been worked out, refined, made pure. Then it'll be gold—life—for those who can accept it. It's what keeps the body of Christ hot—or the absence of which keeps it cool.

---

[5] Matthew 8.18-27; 1 Kings 19.19-21
[6] Revelation 3.18

FOLLOWING THE LAMB
...wherever He goes

Of course it's his plan that what he has put in us is refined and does bear fruit. We're simply to follow, and as we do he works it all out. *The Lord will fulfil his purpose for us.*[7]

As Jesus strikes out in a new direction towards Jerusalem, his disciples follow, even if in ignorance and fear. At this stage they haven't a chance to understand; they're following in their own strength, for this is before Pentecost.

Chapter One - Jesus, up to Caesarea Philippi
(Mark 1-8)

He would later urge his disciples to wait for the power from on high; they too would need the same empowering.

The writers of the New Testament often use Old Testament figures to compare with Jesus. He's the prophet Moses foresaw, Isaiah's servant figure, Daniel's messiah and the king of many Psalms. He's a new Adam, a new Moses and a new David. As already noted the calling of the disciples resonates with the calling of Elisha, and before Jesus even reaches the Jordan to be baptised, Mark compares John the Baptist with Elijah, who like John wore camel's hair clothes and a leather belt.[8]

Jesus' ministry could only begin once he had been baptised in the Holy Spirit at the river Jordan; even he

---

[7] Psalm 138.8
[8] Mark 1.6, cf 2 Kings 1.8

FOLLOWING THE LAMB
...wherever He goes

didn't bear any fruit without first receiving 'the gift the Father had promised.'[9] (Knowing first-hand the necessity of the Spirit's empowering, he would later urge his disciples to wait for the power from on high;[10] they too would need the same empowering.)

The Holy Spirit now leads him out to the desert to be tempted by Satan. The words his heavenly father had just spoken to him in such an intimate and encouraging way as he rose from the baptismal waters, *This is my son whom I love, with him I am well pleased,*[11] now seem long ago as he embarks upon his ordeal face to face with Satan.

Emerging undamaged from 40 days in the wilderness his work begins in earnest. The word 'immediately' litters Mark's account of Jesus' early ministry. Translators, wary of its overuse, often change it to something else (e.g. 'at once'), yet it's there for a reason and his ministry, once begun, is going to be full of action without much let-up. This was Jesus' way, and we can find it our way too. Again, not the immature rushing around of an excited child—we need to get over that—but the seriousness of work coming from God. The call is deep and the work urgent.

Those following Jesus can often sense an anticipation of his imminent return. They can no longer live with a

---

[9] Acts 1.4
[10] Acts 1.8
[11] Mark 1.11

FOLLOWING THE LAMB
...wherever He goes

merely lateral view of time. Even if it shouldn't happen within their lifetime it surely is a very close event, as though somehow it always about to happen—it's just around the corner. He is coming back, we glimpse the urgency of the work, and the 'immediately's' of Jesus ministry echo in our own.

Now equipped, Jesus preaches the kingdom of God and busily travels from meeting to meeting and crowd to crowd. He's aware of his kingship though he knows it will be a funny sort of glory that comes with it, and an even funnier throne. He teaches in the synagogues and causes a stir, for he's teaching with such authority, not as the teachers of the law, those who had studied all their lives.[12] He teaches differently from others because he's carrying something different: something that didn't come from human learning but from encounter with God.

After ministering late into the evening he wakes very early the next morning to go and be alone,[13] receiving strength and revelation for the day ahead, feeding from relationship rather than books, God's words not men's opinions.

The next two or three years are spent busily in and around Galilee, healing, collecting and training disciples, casting out demons, ministering to the crowds and enjoying a busy and fruitful time of

---

[12] **Mark 1.22**
[13] **Mark 1.34-35**

ministry, bringing the kingdom of God wherever he goes. He grows in popularity—at least among the masses.

Shared experience

So far at least, Jesus' ministry follows a pattern that today's charismatics and pentecostals may easily relate to: the years of waiting, the call and equipping of the Holy Spirit, the affirmation from God (even if not from men), and then the time of testing, where the call is put through the fire and refined, all can echo in our own experiences. Even the healings, miracles, divine provisions and authority over demonic spirits (as well as rejection by 'religious' people) resonate with some of our early experiences, as we learn to live out of what he has put deep within us, often making mistakes, but keen nevertheless to reach out and see folk healed and set free.

After these initial exhilarating months and years in Galilee (full of teaching and demonstrating the kingdom of God, quickly passed over here though forming the bulk of the central sections of the gospels), during which Jesus plays down his identity and all speculation about him being Messiah, he confronts his disciples at Caesarea Philippi. *Who do men say that I am* He asks Peter. *You are the Christ (Messiah)* exclaims Peter,[14] excited by the revelation he's receiving. *You're right, Peter—yet you didn't see*

> Jesus' ministry follows a pattern that today's charismatics and pentecostals find it easy to relate to.

---

[14] Mark 8.29-30

FOLLOWING THE LAMB
...wherever He goes

that for yourself, my Father revealed it to you! replies Jesus. Peter follows up by blurting out something about Jesus not going down to Jerusalem and Jesus rebukes him—that bit wasn't from heaven.

Peter's insight is the signal to Jesus that it's time to turn away from Galilee, and head down to Jerusalem where the final act in the drama will be played out.

After climbing a mountain and encountering God's glory, encouraged by more affirming words from his Father and getting human support too, from Moses and Elijah, he's already making the shift from revival minister to sacrificial Lamb.

So they set out on the road and head south—Jesus leading, the disciples amazed, and others who are following, afraid.

Chapter Two - the Journey (Mark 8.22 - 10.52)

And a highway will be there; it will be called the Way of Holiness.[15]

In your unfailing love you will lead the people you have redeemed.[16]

---

[15] Isaiah 35.8
[16] Exodus 15.13

FOLLOWING THE LAMB
...wherever He goes

Jesus continues resolutely on his way, and though the disciples faithfully follow, the journey to Jerusalem adds little to their understanding of what's to come. Jesus tells them clearly where he's going and why at least three times, but they have no ears to hear.

Jesus heals the sick he meets on the way, and his Father watches over him as he has watched over him his whole life. As he journeys on, we may continue to draw parallels between his walk and ours. Understanding for the disciples, that Jesus was modelling obedience and faith, and that this one day would become their journey too, was still some way off.

In Protection

He would willingly yield himself to the authorities.

Jesus was accustomed to the benefits of his heavenly Father's protection. He kept him in safety when Herod slaughtered the baby boys, by sending an angel to warn Joseph thus enabling them to flee to safety.[17]

After his first sermon in the synagogue at Nazareth, the Jews again tried to kill him. *They .... took him to the brow of the hill on which the town was built, in order to throw him down the cliff. But he walked right through the crowd and went on his way.*[18]

---

[17] Matthew 2.13-15
[18] Luke 4.29-30

FOLLOWING THE LAMB
...wherever He goes

Then, when Jesus attended the Feast of Tabernacles, *they tried to seize him, but no-one laid a hand on him, because his time had not yet come.*[19]

We see others, before and since, walk in the same protection: Moses' was saved from Pharaoh's slaughter of the Hebrew babies as Jesus would later be saved from Herod's, God watched over Daniel's friends when they remained obedient and faithful, saving them from the fire, as Daniel himself would be saved from the lions. Rahab and the spies were spared death, Joseph was liberated from prison, a whale rescued Jonah, Paul escaped the city in a basket and Peter walked free when the church rose up in prayer.

His Father has been watching over him his whole life, during his birth, childhood and early adulthood, through his time of ministry in Galilee, and now as he journeys south, towards the lion's den, where the religious authorities were waiting for him. When he is finally arrested it is clear that this is part of the plan – the time had now come – and he would willingly yield himself to the authorities: no one takes him by force. To make this even clearer, as he is arrested the detachment of soldiers who have come to take him fall backwards.[20] Jesus is in charge.

---

[19] John 7.30
[20] John 18.4-6

FOLLOWING THE LAMB
...wherever He goes

Our job — His job

Above all else, guard your heart.

Our job (just as it was Jesus' job) is to lay down our own agendas and desires, instead choosing to believe what God has said, following step by step. We give up our rights, privileges and points of view, instead now finding our joy, drive and very reason for living in him, allowing him to watch over, protect and provide along the way. We are to keep our attitudes and relationships right. *Above all else, guard your heart* the writer of Proverbs warns us.[21] *Above all else.* This will become a challenge for Jesus too as he now nears the end of his earthly journey.[22]

Jesus seems unperturbed at the horror of what lies ahead, or by his own disciples' inability to hear what he is teaching them. He walks in peace. He is even excited when his disciples return from mission declaring 'It works!' Of course he will face the personal cost in Gethsemane, but this is not his day by day demeanour as he travels to Jerusalem continuing to teach his disciples.

We, like he, delight in his Protection and Provision

It is indeed a great joy to follow Jesus.

Moses sang a song after the Red Sea parted, Hannah sang a song after her barrenness was miraculously healed, and Mary and Zechariah burst into prophetic verse following the events surrounding the births of

---

[21] Proverbs 4.23
[22] See Five Smooth Stones in the same series of short courses for more on this.

FOLLOWING THE LAMB
...wherever He goes

their respective baby boys. Joy, often expressed in music, is a natural response to God's goodness in our lives.

New moves of God in the Church over past centuries produced new songs from the hearts of Jesus' followers. When we see God's strong hand upon our circumstances we sing songs from the bottom of our hearts—not just because of what God has done but because God's faithfulness has been proven yet again. He is real and he is true—despite us, not because of us. It is indeed a great joy to follow Jesus, and as his promises and faithfulness are proven time and time again.

As I write this today, for example, I reflect on God's recent financial provision. I recently received three gifts of equal size, equally unexpected and equally necessary, and equally spaced (one per month for three months). They arrived without the givers knowing anything about my needs or the other gifts. My first response in each case was to jump in the air with delight at God's faithfulness, his intimate knowledge of what we need and his Father's heart towards us. I jumped not primarily because he met my need, but because once again he'd shown himself to be the essence of faithfulness and love and trustworthiness: he is who he says he is; and he is true to what he says he will do.

His provision—of everything, not just finance: power, miracles, grace—is always there for his disciples. As we follow, he watches and provides. *Our* job is to stick close to him; *his* job is to supply all we need.

Protection on Mission in Africa

> God watches over us no matter where he sends us, no matter what we walk through.

A few weeks before leaving for our first mission to Rwanda, which we'd planned by the clear leading of the Holy Spirit (and for which he had provided miraculously), I awoke in the night in a cold sweat. I had been reading up on the genocide there some years earlier and my mind was full of images of slaughter by machete: during 100 days, over 850,000 people were brutally murdered by fellow citizens. *Why on earth am I going there?* Fear came upon me and I battled for some time that night before peace finally fell. If God were taking me there then it would be the safest place for me to be.

Actually Rwanda is now as safe as anywhere in Africa, and my fears were completely unjustified. (Isn't that so often the case with fear—False Expectation Appearing Real?) Whilst there however I wrestled with some other obviously demonic 'stuff'. My voice began going after just a few days teaching. A Rwandan Anglican bishop shared that he and his fellow bishops constantly struggled against such symptoms and he put it down to the spiritual warfare in what he considered to be a key African nation. For decades, he explained, Rwanda had experienced powerful revivals and, often hot on their heels, horrible civil wars and genocides.

FOLLOWING THE LAMB
...wherever He goes

In the early hours of one morning, I tried to get out of bed. As I turned my body to rise, my head smashed against the solid wooden top of a chair upright (African furniture is solid and heavy). Not knowing what had hit me (it felt like I had just received a blow out of nowhere), I clutched my head, which was in considerable pain. It had happened out of the blue and I sat on the edge of my bed, bewildered for a few moments. I had thought I was fairly safe in my bedroom alone in the early hours of the morning! I cleaned up the dripping blood and bandaged my head.

Determined not to make much of it (and remembering Wigglesworth's famous episode in his bedroom)[23] I joked about it to the delegates the next morning.

There was a humorous postscript when, the following night, I awoke having felt the bed move, to see the curtain blowing in through an open window. 'Oh. It's only you,' I thought, in my semi-awake state, turned over and went back to sleep. In the morning we discovered there had been a small earthquake not far away.

My point is not to glorify the enemy or waste any time dwelling on his ways (these were in any case minor things), but to show how God watches over us no

---

[23] The story goes, now well-known and rather over-used, that Smith Wigglesworth was in bed when he heard a noise. When he turned and saw it was Satan he nonchalantly said to him: "Oh it's only you", turned over and went back to sleep.

matter where he sends us, no matter what we walk through. The day before we came home from Rwanda after the powerful two week mission, I heard a voice as clearly as day (not audibly). It said quite unmistakably 'You're not welcome in this country—don't bother coming back.' A little worn down by now, with a fading throat, tiredness and the impact of a visit to the Congo, where the sights and atmosphere made quite an impression our western sensibilities, and now even some stomach pain, my first reaction was to think, 'Well, we're going home tomorrow anyway.' But another voice rose up, equally clearly, 'Richard you have to get on top of this or you will come straight under it when you return.' So I rose up on the inside and fought the fear and negativity. It departed and never returned—I've visited the country many times since and had trouble-free, fruitful missions. What was begun there on that first mission is bearing good lasting fruit as pastors and leaders are growing in their Kingdom ministries.

On mission, following him, he provided finance, protection from fear, health to minister, wisdom against listening to the wrong voices, and fruitfulness in the ministry. Even as we struggled to get through heavy Kigali traffic en route to the airport as we ended the mission, it seemed as though we would miss the plane due to a demonstration in the city blocking traffic. Praying hard (we were keen to get home) the way unexpectedly became clear and we made it onto the plane just in time. On many remarkable missions we've known God's hand on

FOLLOWING THE LAMB
...wherever He goes

things in many big and not-so-big ways. Over many missions to Africa and India and beyond, we've never had disunity, serious illness, logistical failures or accidents to speak of.

God doesn't say 'Become a Christian and I will be with you whatever you decide to do.'; rather he says 'Follow me, and I will be with you wherever I lead you. Just as I was with Jesus.' When we know God is with us we can rise up, overcome whatever might seek to undermine our work, and follow.

The world says 'See and believe', faith says 'Believe and you shall see!' *Go and make disciples of all nations...and surely I am with you always.*[24] The going comes first, then the miracle. Elijah, for instance, was sent to the Kerith ravine, and only once he'd arrived there did he see the miracle of provision.

We're to live by faith, not by sight, so we must be led by his word to us (for it's the word that is the lamp unto our feet), which produces the faith to step out despite not yet seeing. When we follow him we will often not understand where the step will lead us or what will come next. It's ok, have faith.

We're to walk as Jesus walked, trusting out father in heaven for protection, provision and everything else we will need.

---

[24] Matthew 28.19-20

FOLLOWING THE LAMB
...wherever He goes

Spiritual blindness

> *Jesus promised that streams of living water would flow from within us.*

Jesus continued on his way to Jerusalem under his Father's watchful eye. Between Galilee and Jerusalem he heals two men of physical blindness, and between the healings he tells the disciples what is going to happen to him and they still don't seem to hear it. This whole passage[25] is about spiritual blindness, the two stories of physical blindness acting as clues to point to what is between them: the spiritual blindness of the disciples.

The first man is healed at Bethsaida[26]—just before the transfiguration and the decision to turn and head south for Jerusalem but Mark's real purpose is made clear by following it with the account of Peter coming to a place of clear-sightedness about who Jesus is.[27] The blind man's eyes were fully opened after first seeing people like trees; Peter sees Jesus is the Christ while others only get a partial understanding of who he is.

Following Peter's revelation, Jesus begins to teach the disciples 'I'm going to suffer at the hands of the religious people, be killed and then rise again.' As if the meaning of this isn't quite apparent, Mark adds *He spoke plainly about this.*[28] Yet Peter, who has just 'seen' that Jesus is indeed the Messiah, takes Jesus to

---

[25] Mark 8.22 - 10.52
[26] Mark 8.22-26
[27] Mark 8.27-30
[28] Mark 8.32

FOLLOWING THE LAMB
...wherever He goes

one side to talk him out of going on. Jesus rebuked Peter—one moment he's speaking great revelation, the next he's the mouthpiece of Satan. *"Get behind me, Satan!" he said, "you do not have in mind the things of God, but the things of men."*[29]

Man can be used to utter great mysteries and revelations from God and yet can be the devil's mouthpiece in the next breath. The power of God will fill Peter in a new way at Pentecost, and enable even greater revelations about God and who Jesus really is.

Jesus promised that *streams of living water* (not just occasional revelations) *would flow from within us,*[30] he said nothing about a mixture, yet until we train it we're still as likely to use our mouth in the wrong way—and Jesus' brother James, even post-Pentecost, speaks of the possibility that we will speak not just revelations from heaven but: *Out of the same mouth come praise and cursing.*[31]

Jesus continues to speak plainly: *If anyone would come after me, he must deny himself, and take up his cross and follow me. For whoever wants to save his life will lose it, but whoever loses his life for me and for the gospel will save it. What good is it for a man to gain the whole world yet forfeit his soul?*[32]

---

[29] Mark 8.33
[30] John 7.38
[31] James 3.10
[32] Mark 8.34-35

FOLLOWING THE LAMB
...wherever He goes

After the transfiguration Jesus speaks for a second time to them about what is going to happen to him: *"The Son of Man is going to be betrayed into the hands of men. They will kill him, and after three days he will rise."* But they did not understand what he meant and were afraid to ask him about it.[33]

He's telling them in simple words what is going to happen and again they miss it: instead, as they walk along the road towards Capernaum they argue among themselves about who is the greatest.[34]

As they continue towards Jerusalem Jesus teaches about the Kingdom, faces the Pharisees who are increasingly attempting now to catch him out, challenges the rich young ruler with his love of money despite his devotion to other aspects of Jewish teaching, and makes a third attempt to communicate to his disciples what will happen. *"We are going up to Jerusalem,"* he said, *"and the Son of Man will be betrayed to the chief priests and teachers of the law. They will condemn him to death and will hand him over to the Gentiles, who will mock him and spit on him, flog him and kill him. Three days later he will rise."*[35] Here is another bald statement to his spiritually blind disciples about what's ahead, and as if their slowness needed underlining, the next passage is about James and John asking for special privileges in the Kingdom. Jesus asks them if they really understand what they're

---

[33] Mark 9.31-32
[34] Mark 9.33-35
[35] Mark 10.33-34

asking—can they drink from the same cup he will drink with? *We can,* they confidently answer. Can they really!?

They will understand one day. For now, Jesus rebukes them for seeking position in the Kingdom.

Just as it isn't our job to decide our place in the life to come neither is it our job to decide where we sit in the body, or in ministry. These are matters for God. We are simply to step out in the works prepared in advance for us to walk into.[36] Again: it's God's responsibility to show us where to walk; it's our responsibility to walk there.

Selfish ambition

The disciples wouldn't be the last to allow their personal ambition to obstruct God's purposes for their lives. It's not for us to raise ourselves up or to seek status in the kingdom. Jesus says, those who are first will be last and those who are last will find themselves first - *for even the Son of Man did not come to be served but to serve.*[37] Selfishly seeking position in the body opens the door to the enemy into our lives and into the church.

> Selfishly seeking position in the body opens the door to the enemy into our lives and into the church.

Elsewhere in the New Testament we are warned against taking note of 'wisdom' from sources where

---

[36] Ephesians 2.10
[37] Mark 10.43-45

selfish ambition is present.[38] Rather, James says, it's the wisdom from those with *pure, peace loving, considerate, submissive hearts, full of mercy and good fruit* that is from heaven and therefore to be listened to. This can help us weigh up even apparently helpful words people say to us, and can help us see why sometimes our great wisdom isn't received in the body in the way we think it ought to be![39]

If selfish ambition isn't dealt with in our own lives God will be unable to use us as he wants. We will find ourselves struggling against leadership in the body, and ultimately against God himself. We won't understand why, and will blame anything or anybody but ourselves. We can make prophetic statements, preach sermons and we can write books, but will only benefit the body of Christ, bearing fruit as he wants us to, when our hearts are free from these things and we're truly seeking to be used only in the way God chooses, even willing to be cast aside if that is his will for us.

Of course it's hard to recognise selfish ambition in ourselves; such is the nature of all deception. The Holy Spirit will attempt to show us, however, and if we don't accept it God provides others - maybe from among those who have walked ahead of us - to help us see. If we still don't see it then we can sometimes

---

[38] James 3.13-18
[39] See *Five Smooth Stones*, a short course in this series.

find doors shutting and circumstances working against us. He will have his way.

As Jesus progresses towards the climax of his mission in Jerusalem he doesn't allow anything to drag him off course. He's walking towards the cross and nothing will stop him.

Now Bartimaeus is healed of his (physical) blindness and Jesus will enter Jerusalem on the colt, in triumph, at least for now, and to the delight of the crowds.[40]

Chapter Three - The Great Project

As the time approached for him to be taken up to heaven, Jesus resolutely set out for Jerusalem[41]

But Jesus made no reply, not even to a single charge— to the great amazement of the governor.[42]

We may never fully comprehend the way Jesus walked in the last days before he was crucified. He is a man, and he walked to his death, yet with great poise. He is aware of the pain that lies ahead yet never allows the prospect of the agony to deter him from maintaining his peace and confidence - before men and before God. At every step along the journey

…e is aware of the pain that lies ahead yet never allows the prospect of the ony to deter him rom maintaining his peace and confidence.

---

[40] Mark 10.46-52
[41] Luke 9.51
[42] Matthew 27.14

he knows who he is and what he is doing; he has full confidence in his Father, trusts him implicitly and *fixes his stare on the joy beyond the cross.*[43] He is moving in the power of the Holy Spirit, and having travelled so far will finish what he has come to do.

No wonder then that he stands out from the men around him. When he comes before Pilate we see two kingdoms clashing: the world and worldly ways meeting the king of the kingdom of God, where things are upside down, often not quite what they seem, where different rules seem to apply. In John's account of the meeting this is portrayed so clearly.[44] Who is really the powerful one here? The one to whom the world attributes authority, the one who has the authority to put the prisoner to death, or the prisoner who is bound and apparently at the mercy of the others' decision? Is it the uniformed judge or the bound victim? Which of the two men knows true freedom, true joy?

Matthew's perspective of the encounter between Jesus and Pilate ... provides a contrast between one who walks fearing God and the other whose fears are grounded in the world around him.

Jesus before Pilate (Matthew's account)

Meanwhile Jesus stood before the governor, and the governor asked him, "Are you the king of the Jews?"

"Yes, it is as you say," Jesus replied.

When he was accused by the chief priests and the elders, he gave no answer. Then Pilate asked him,

---

[43] **Hebrews 12.2 (paraphrased)**
[44] **John 19**

FOLLOWING THE LAMB
...wherever He goes

"Don't you hear the testimony they are bringing against you?" But Jesus made no reply, not even to a single charge—to the great amazement of the governor.

Now it was the governor's custom at the Feast to release a prisoner chosen by the crowd. At that time they had a notorious prisoner, called Barabbas. So when the crowd had gathered, Pilate asked them, "Which one do you want me to release to you: Barabbas, or Jesus who is called Christ?" For he knew it was out of envy that they had handed Jesus over to him.

While Pilate was sitting on the judge's seat, his wife sent him this message: "Don't have anything to do with that innocent man, for I have suffered a great deal today in a dream because of him."

But the chief priests and the elders persuaded the crowd to ask for Barabbas and to have Jesus executed.

"Which of the two do you want me to release to you?" asked the governor.

"Barabbas," they answered.

"What shall I do, then, with Jesus who is called Christ?" Pilate asked.

They all answered, "Crucify him!"

"Why? What crime has he committed?" asked Pilate.

But they shouted all the louder, "Crucify him!"

FOLLOWING THE LAMB
...wherever He goes

When Pilate saw that he was getting nowhere, but that instead an uproar was starting, he took water and washed his hands in front of the crowd. "I am innocent of this man's blood," he said. "It is your responsibility!"

All the people answered, "Let his blood be on us and on our children!" — A Curse

Then he released Barabbas to them. But he had Jesus flogged, and handed him over to be crucified.[45]

Matthew's perspective of the encounter between Jesus and Pilate, like John's, reveals a lot about how the two men are walking. It contrasts one who fears God and another whose fears are grounded in the world around him. The single-minded man of vision and of purpose, with confidence in what lies ahead no matter what personal cost he has to face, against the one who lives self-protectively, more afraid of what men say than of any eternal perspective. One following God and the other the crowd.

What does each man believe in? What or who do they trust? What are they motivated, moved by? What do they fear? Who do they listen to?

We're told that when the chief priests and elders accuse Jesus he gives no reply.[46] He is so set on his goal that he chooses not to sink to the level of those accusing him. He knows for certain that it matters

---

[45] Matthew 27.11-26
[46] Matthew 27.12b

FOLLOWING THE LAMB
...wherever He goes

more what God thinks of him than what any man does.

How difficult it is when we are accused! We develop such neat strategies to protect ourselves from others' criticism yet Christ shows us the way: he has justified us and we need never seek to justify or defend ourselves. If we're walking with Jesus and following him wherever he goes then we are bound to face accusation, even persecution,[47] yet we're never to defend ourselves.

It is hard for Jesus to be accused by the very people he has come to save. Yet he chooses to remain in a place of righteousness. That is, he lives first in the place his Father has put him. Justifying himself before them would bring him down to their level. But he came to bring us up to his.

The height from which we've fallen

If we are born again of the Spirit we are *seated with him in the heavenly realms.*[48] We also are not to leave that place in order to hold discussions with those who accuse us, plot against us or persecute us.[49] When we walk confidently in his righteousness we don't need to descend to the level of any who seek, wittingly or otherwise, to undermine the work of the kingdom.

When we walk confidently in his righteousness we don't need to descend to the level of any who seek, wittingly or otherwise, to undermine the work of the kingdom.

---

[47] Luke 21.12; John 15.20
[48] Ephesians 2.6
[49] Interestingly it is the Ephesian church, to whom Paul spoke of their place seated with him in heavenly places, who Jesus tells to remember the height from which they have fallen (Revelation 2.5 cf Ephesians 2.6))

FOLLOWING THE LAMB
...wherever He goes

When we walk in obedience, when we follow the Lamb, we can echo the psalmist: *Contend O Lord with those who contend with me; fight against those who fight against me. Take up shield and buckler; arise and come to my aid.*[50] Of course, we don't fight flesh and blood but powers and principalities—the problem is that it is through people that the powers and principalities so often find expression. All the more reason not to engage in arguments with those who misunderstand or even oppose us. When there is a wrong spirit operating in someone's life we will not win any argument.

In his letter to the Romans Paul says something similar: *Do not take revenge, my friends, but leave room for God's wrath, for it is written: "It is mine to avenge; I will repay," says the Lord.*[51] When we try to justify ourselves, avenge our accusers or use reason to contend with those who come against us, we will find ourselves trying to beat flesh with flesh. God is big enough to sort out the other people. The Spirit will always overcome the flesh—or, to put it another way, doing something God's way will always accomplish his kingdom purpose.

I'm not coming down!

As Jesus stood before Pilate, did he identify with Nehemiah? He'd have known well the account of the

> *Sanballat didn't give up easily, but Nehemiah remained unmoved.*

---

[50] Psalm 35.1-2
[51] Romans 12.19

returning exiles rebuilding the walls of Jerusalem and Sanballat coming to Nehemiah, very reasonably (or so it appeared), to ask him for a meeting. Nehemiah immediately saw through the approach: *...they were scheming to harm me; so I sent messengers to them with this reply: "I am carrying on a great project and cannot go down. Why should the work stop while I leave it and go down to you?"*[52]

Sanballat didn't give up easily, but Nehemiah remained unmoved: *Four times they sent me the same message, and each time I gave them the same answer.*[53] — he's not fooled for a moment. How many of us are though? The attempt to undermine that which God has set before us, masquerading as a very reasonable enquiry, tempts us to come down from the place where Christ has put us to engage in a conversation designed to stall us. The person through whom the reasonable enquiry comes may or may not have any notion as to what is happening, but the man or woman engaged on 'a great project' must learn that these things are spiritually discerned.

Jesus was also carrying on a great project. He similarly refused to go down from the place where his Father had put him. He too was Kingdom building and was being similarly baited. It would have appeared very reasonable for Nehemiah to have met Sanballat as requested, and there he could have *reasonably*

---

[52] **Nehemiah 6.2-3**
[53] **Nehemiah 6.4**

explained to Sanballat his authority to do what he was doing, as it would have been reasonable for Christ to defend his ministry to the religious leaders and Roman authorities.

But Nehemiah saw through it and his great project wasn't held up. Nor did Jesus reply to the accusations made against him, for, as Nehemiah had done, he discerned the spirit behind the interruptions and walked in the fear of God, not man.

So Jesus doesn't engage in discussion or accuse Pilate of harbouring a wrong spirit, nor does he attempt to persuade Pilate of the reality of the matter or put himself under Pilate's judgment. What he does is to walk in an opposite way to Pilate, in the fear of the Lord, meekly[54] and supremely confident in his Father, yielding to whatever they would do to him, knowing that the Kingdom operates differently from the world, and trusting his Father to exercise supreme lordship over the world and those in it. He walks in perfect humility, not judging or allowing himself to be under any man's judgment.

A fool For Christ

This is the Kingdom way, the way of righteousness, the way of the Spirit. If Nehemiah and Jesus valued the call of God on their lives more than anything else, those coming after Jesus would too. Paul, for example,

He is unmoved by what men think.

---

[54] For meekness does not equal weakness – rather 'strength under control'

speaks of the life of an apostle, the life spent as a fool for Christ, *We are weak, but you are strong! You are honoured but we are dishonoured! To this very hour we go hungry and thirsty, we are in rags, we are brutally treated, we are homeless. We work hard with our own hands. When we are cursed, we bless; when we are persecuted, we endure it; when we are slandered, we answer kindly. Up to this moment we have become the scum of the earth, the refuse of the world.*[55]

He is unmoved by what men think, *I care very little if I am judged by you or by any human court; indeed, I do not even judge myself. My conscience is clear, but that does not make me innocent. It is the Lord who judges me.*[56] He doesn't claim to have yet been perfected but knows his place — he has been justified by Christ and it is God alone who will judge him. He is willing to be considered rubbish by men provided he fulfils that which God asks of him. He is clear too of how others should see him: *...men ought to regard us as servants of Christ and as those entrusted with the secret things of God.*[57] That they don't is not going to hold up his work, for he like Nehemiah is engaged on a great project.

That Jesus makes no reply at all amazes Pilate.[58] He isn't used to prisoners having nothing to say for themselves. He asks the crowd if they want to release

---

[55] 1 Corinthians 4.10-13
[56] 1 Corinthians 4.3-4
[57] 1 Corinthians 4.1
[58] Matthew 27.14

FOLLOWING THE LAMB
...wherever He goes

Jesus or Barabbas and they choose Barabbas, and what follows is a picture of a man seeking to protect his life contrasted with one who is about lose his; one who is grasping at his own human reason and human instincts, the other walking according to wisdom from heaven. Both have opportunities to hear and to act accordingly.

Wisdom from heaven

> *The moment he decides to come down, his great project is lost.*

Pilate's chance to hear 'wisdom from heaven' came when his wife advised him to have nothing to do with Jesus. *Don't have anything to do with that innocent man, for I have suffered a great deal today in a dream because of him.*[59] Pilate didn't listen to her, didn't seem to hear what she says about Jesus, and continues to engage with the crowd, asking them now what they want.

Pilate gave room to the voices that were not of God—not wisdom from heaven. The point at which he errs isn't when he washes his hands in the basin, but as he entertained the voice of the crowd. Had he listened to his wife and at this point declined to 'go down' and engage with the crowd, he could have walked in the wisdom he'd received and released Jesus, but the moment he began debating with those who opposed this way ahead he opened the door, as it were, to instability and double-mindedness.

---

[59] Matthew 27.19

FOLLOWING THE LAMB
...wherever He goes

This is what James describes when he tells us to ask for wisdom if we need it, and that God will give it. *But, he continues, when he asks, he must believe and not doubt, because he who doubts is like a wave of the sea, blown and tossed by the wind. That man should not think he will receive anything from the Lord; he is a double-minded man, unstable in all he does.*[60]

Pilate continues to debate with the crowd: *Which of the two do you want me to release?*[61] When the crowd cries *Crucify him!* Pilate engages them in discussion *Why? What crime has he committed?* But all they do is shout all the louder. They always will. In engaging with the wrong voices Pilate has stirred them up and he will of course never persuade them otherwise. His only way of releasing Jesus was to listen to his wife (representing in our cameo here, the Holy Spirit) and refusing to banter with the crowd or anyone else. The moment he decides to come down, his great project is lost.

Jesus meanwhile demonstrates the exact opposite way. There is no double-mindedness in him; his great project will not be stopped for anyone. He is secure in what his Father in heaven has called him to do, he is going to see it through whatever anyone says or does, and so he refuses to come down and certainly won't risk stirring the flesh of those around him. Any

---

[60] James 1.6-8
[61] Matthew 27.21

vindication required will come from the Father at the right time.

In Christ Jesus

Now that we have been placed into Christ, seated in heavenly places, this is where we can remain. We're not to leave this place, not even to answer our accusers or to be moved by any other distraction. God will always vindicate us, he has already justified us and even has given us the grace required to stay put – always. Christ's righteousness is now ours, and the place he has put us *is* the place of righteousness. To remain here is the right thing to do—what used to appear reasonable and proper may well now be foolishness. To *not* answer back, *not* engage in argument, *not* analyse the accusations and respond to them point by point, may be the difficult thing to do but is essential if we are to stay true to our call to follow him. To seek first his Kingdom and his righteousness will always mean remaining in the place he has put us rather than going down. We're also engaged in a great project.

> *We're also engaged in a great project.*

Isaiah spoke of a highway of holiness: *And a highway will be there; it will be called the Way of Holiness. The unclean will not journey on it; it will be for those who walk in that Way; wicked fools will not go about on it. No lion will be there, nor will any ferocious beast get up* on it; they will not be found there. But only the redeemed will walk there.'[62]

The highway Isaiah describes is the highway Jesus walked and the highway he made possible for us to walk. This is not a 'religious' route, where everything is neat and tidy and comfortable—it wasn't for Jesus and it isn't for us. It's a place of obedience, of sacrifice, of devotion and of service. It's also a place of safety, joy, peace and fruitfulness. It can be hard, and exhilarating; it is tough but we wouldn't turn back once we've embarked on it. It's a narrow way, one which the world (even the Christian world sometimes) has turned its back upon, yet it's the only way described in the Bible and it's the only way Jesus walked, and once it becomes our way we desire no other.

Spiritual growth

All spiritual growth will, one way or another, be a result of following Jesus. Seeking to be led by doctrine, theology, our own thinking, good works, or emulating Jesus in our own strength, will not result in the full extent of growth God intends for us. These things may strengthen our minds, emotions and even wills, they may bring understanding and many other worthy things. There is nothing necessarily wrong with them. Yet it is only in becoming disciples,

spiritual growth will, one way or another, be a result of following Jesus.

---

[62] Isaiah 35.8-9

following him, that we can bear the fruit he intends for us to bear.

We are in danger of living in reaction to one end or other of man-made continuums. For instance, 'conservative' spirituality wants to avoid an over-emphasis on the natural world. It will avoid at all costs placing man in the place where God should be. Christians at this end of the spectrum will shy away from merely ethical Christianity. They avoid being *too earthly use to be of any heavenly good.* At the other end however, 'liberal' Christians seek to avoid at all costs an over-emphasis on miracles, demons and dogmatic approaches to biblical interpretation. They resist what they see as super-spirituality and dualistic attitudes. They see conservatives as *too heavenly good to be of any earthly use.*

John McKay in **When the Veil is Taken Away**[63] avoids debating the merits of either end of the continuum but suggests that once filled with the Spirit of God we're lifted above this tension of right or left (and indeed every other), empowered to see the truth now through revelation (the Spirit of God revealing the word of God).

I'd like to add—in the context of this short course—that it is as we follow Jesus, in relationship with him, trusting him and what he says rather than (necessarily) our own natural instincts, that we avoid

---

[63] Published by The Way of the Spirit

the error of either pole and we can avoid reactionary lurches. In this way the conflict between the two poles is left behind as priority is given to hearing what God says. We don't have to take an intellectual stance for we find our way in him, not through blind obedience and silliness but through rich relationship and deep commitment to God and his kingdom purposes, where our lives make sense and find meaning in and out of our relationship with him as we learn to hear him and follow. We can avoid the wrong sort of dogma and shallow spirituality just as we can avoid unbelief and demythologising the Bible[64] by choosing to pursue relationship with Jesus (enabled by the Holy Spirit alone) whatever the cost.

Many search for more meaning and depth to their Christian lives. It is perhaps a common error to look elsewhere than to God himself to make up this lack. *'Come near to me and I will come near to you.'*[65] Relationship with him— through the word by the Spirit (even when not directly, then certainly indirectly: always resonating with the witness of the entire revelation of God's dealings with men from Genesis through to Revelation)—is the way through the fundamentalist/intellectual/ethical morass.

To need to understand everything God says to us is to limit God to the size of our intellect. If we don't understand then we don't follow. We can live our

---

[64] I mean by demythologising: reducing God's miraculous interventions into the world to natural phenomena, explainable through reason and scientific advancement.
[65] James 4.8

lives reducing God to the level of our own intellect which, however large and capable, will never reach God, define God or adequately understand him.

So following him really does become a matter of faith. Hence the celebrations every time his faithfulness to what he says—in relationship—is proved again. It's beyond our understanding but he is good and true to his word!

Chapter Four - The Aroma of Christ

AND THE NEW SONG

We are to continue Jesus' ministry here on earth.

'And they sang a new song before the throne and before the four living creatures and the elders...they follow the Lamb wherever he goes.'[66]

Wherever Jesus went he took the Kingdom. He preached the Kingdom, and he demonstrated the Kingdom. Wherever he went he took light and life. His light shone on darkness and it brought healing, restored relationships and revived people's relationships with God. Demons were cast out, for where there is light, darkness cannot survive. Just as when a light switch is turned on the darkness flees, so where Jesus went the darkness had to go.

---

[66] Revelation 14.3-4

FOLLOWING THE LAMB
...wherever He goes

As we've seen, where Jesus walked in obedience, guarding his heart, so the Kingdom broke out around him. It cost Jesus to remain in that place where he overcame every human temptation to come down from the place of righteousness. In his humanity he chose to submit to the Holy Spirit's lead in his life and he refused to come down from the place his Father had put him.

When we choose to stay where Christ has put us we too will see his life around us. *'But thanks be to God, who always leads us in triumphal procession in Christ and through us spreads everywhere the fragrance of the knowledge of him. For we are the aroma of Christ among those who are saved and those who are perishing.'*[67]

This is such an exciting verse. Jesus has made provision for our weakness and done everything for us to overcome and to walk in victory. When we do choose to avail ourselves of his provision and make the right choices, overcoming as Jesus overcame, then as we go into the world we take his aroma—his fragrance: the Kingdom. The fruit of the Holy Spirit will increasingly be borne in our lives, as a by-product.

We cannot make anything happen ourselves. We can't heal, make the demons depart, or bring his eternal Kingdom life, but what Paul is saying here is that we

---

[67] 2Corinthians 2.14

FOLLOWING THE LAMB
...wherever He goes

don't have to—what we're to do is to live a life seeking to overcome and then we will take his life wherever we go, taking his authority and his kingdom. Seek first the kingdom and his righteousness and all these things will be added unto you.

As Christians we sometimes try to be holy, good people, like Jesus. However commendable it may be to attempt such a thing, it's impossible. We just can't do it! Have you tried recently? It can work for short spells, sometimes, but though we can fool some of the people some of the time we can't fool God—ever. He is not to be mocked. No, we can't emulate Jesus, nor are we meant to—at least not in our own strength. But as we fight in our lives to overcome and to stay in a place of holiness (and it is a fight!), responding to every challenge that comes our way by choosing to believe what God says against every circumstance and contrary voice, then we will (as a by-product) take with us the fragrance of Jesus—the Kingdom—into the dark places.

Staying in the right place, *remaining in him*, can be desperately hard at times, desperately uncomfortable and desperately challenging. Many times if we'd had a choice we would have chosen another path—another way. Yet there is no other.

Through all the learning to overcome, God continues to work through us. Even during the personal times of fighting and struggling God keeps the doors of ministry opportunity open.

FOLLOWING THE LAMB
...wherever He goes

There are times of great joy in overcoming, and of great weariness in having to overcome. When we're flattened there is his grace again, when we need strength there's his word, encouraging sign, changed life or healed body. Never, by the grace of God, does the joy of our salvation have to sink without trace and never need our direction falter.

Recently I was teaching at a weekend conference. We've taught in places where the presence of God and teaching 'flow' has felt stronger, yet we rejoiced to watch people visibly changing over the three days. Their faces altered, some were healed, others were set free of longstanding addictions and wrong thinking about themselves. New impetus and vision was created. It wasn't the teaching that did that—it was the release of life from within us—not our own but the life of the Spirit; that which was also in Jesus.

I rejoice at what God has done in so many who have been part of what God's been doing. I see them gaining strength, overcoming in testing situations, seeing difficult circumstances turned around and finding their place in church as servants in the Kingdom rather than consumers in a pew.

A little while ago a lady came to one of our evening meetings in Norwich for the first time. She was visibly struggling with an ulcerated leg. We didn't teach on healing that evening—actually it was about hearing God. We listened and God spoke directly to many. I later received a call from this lady to say her bandage had fallen off and the leg was healing, totally against everything spoken over it by the doctors. A lady in the college last year was set free from mental illness and dependence on medication. A mute man in India spoke for the first time in his life during the last mission there.

We recently returned from Africa where we saw many physical ailments healed, leaders of churches changed and re-envisioned, hope restored to churches and communities, and 2000 students revived at their university, where genocide was plotted pre-1994. We saw God's kingdom breaking in around us as we spoke what God gave us to speak.

When I saw for the first time this scriptural link between overcoming and carrying the aroma of Christ I was having to overcome in a particular area and wasn't feeling very righteous in the struggle. The following day I went into a meeting with a man whom I'd been attempting to help. Nothing at all about me that morning (as far as I could tell!) was very attractive or Christ-like. Yet after obediently (and somewhat reluctantly) delivering a short scripture I believed God had given me for this man, he rose to his feet, came towards me and wept on my shoulder. The thing I was overcoming was unrelated to this man—but the fact that we're seeking to live the overcoming life is enough to produce the aroma of the fragrance of Christ.

FOLLOWING THE LAMB
...wherever He goes

'Go into all the world...and lo I will be with you always.'[68] Jesus promises his disciples just before returning to heaven. We are to continue Jesus' ministry here on earth. The church is to overcome, by his grace and by his power, and take the kingdom into the entire world. Our job is to believe, walk in obedience and to overcome; his job is to produce the aroma of Christ in and through us! *To him who overcomes I will give the right to eat from the tree of life.*

We will see the kingdom come on earth as it is in heaven when, as we follow him, we look to him for the strength to overcome whatever he may lead us into. It's no good us hiding from the difficulties or avoiding the challenge, as we then fall into religion and/or passivity. No—we're to hitch up our cloaks and step out on the path of following him wherever he goes, setting our faces like flint as he did, watching around us as the light within us overtakes all darkness bringing his kingdom, his rule, his kingship.

God has a new song for the church; it is a new song that brings life and life in all its fullness. It is for those that follow the Lamb.

---

[68] Matthew 28.20

FOLLOWING THE LAMB
...wherever He goes

Postscript

Through my death will come much life.

'*I tell you the truth, unless a grain of wheat falls into the ground and dies, it remains only a single seed. But if it dies, it produces many seeds...Whoever serves me must follow me; and where I am, my servant also will be.*'[69]

Until recently I'd never linked these verses above—despite the fact one follows the other! Just as the disciples didn't hear what Jesus was saying to them on the way down to Jerusalem, so we can decline to hear what he says so blatantly to us.

Jesus is about to begin the final part of his journey to the cross where he will die. His mission has been to the Jews, though out of compassion he has sometimes reached out also to others, Gentiles, who come to him—often expressing more faith in who he is than his own people do.

Some Greeks come and ask if they can talk to him. Though his heart is full of compassion for them, Jesus declines, instead fixing his eyes on what lies ahead. He knows that he is only one person—that unless he fulfils his task of going to the cross, the job of filling the world with the kingdom will never happen. 'If I stay alive I will only be one!' he's saying. 'But if I die

---

[69] John 12.24,26

FOLLOWING THE LAMB
...wherever He goes

the Holy Spirit will be poured out and many, *many* people who come after me will then be filled with the Holy Spirit and each can walk as I have walked. Through my death will come much life.'

Then he says something interesting: *'Whoever serves me must follow me.'* This seems the wrong way round—wouldn't it make more sense to say 'whoever follows me must serve me'?

Many say they want to serve Jesus.

Jesus says those who serve must follow—follow where? He has just talked of falling into the ground and dying. This is where we are to follow!

When we follow the Lamb wherever he goes it inevitably leads to our death. Not execution on the cross maybe, but every day picking up our cross and carrying it—choosing to overcome: temptation, difficult situations in relationships, in families, at work, in ministry, in church, in the world. Choosing to stay in the right place, with Jesus and Nehemiah, will always cost us. Sometimes it will feel like it's costing us everything. We will have to fall into the ground and die.

Just as after Jesus' death he knew resurrection life and multiplication of kingdom life, so *we* will see that life—manifesting around us as we go out into the world, led by him. We will understand what the pre-Pentecost disciples didn't; we'll see what the post-

FOLLOWING THE LAMB
...wherever He goes

Pentecost disciples saw. His life from his church—the kingdom of heaven coming on earth as it is in heaven.

None of us can make anything happen, but all of us can follow the Lamb wherever he goes.

FOLLOWING THE LAMB
...wherever He goes

2.

FOLLOWING THE LAMB PART TWO

STUDY GUIDE

These notes consist of five sets of questions, which, I suggest, can be used over five consecutive meetings. They are ideal to use in a church house-group or existing The Way of the Spirit group or just on your own. Not every question has an answer that can be found in the text (though most can). All questions are designed to stimulate further thought and discussion. Be careful not to get distracted by fruitless theological intricacies or argument! The questions should not require lengthy answers.

1. First, read the relevant part of the booklet (pages 1-9 for week one; 9-17 for week two; 18-23 for week three; 23-38 for week four; 38-46 for week five). Look up and read the Bible passages shown.

FOLLOWING THE LAMB
...wherever He goes

2. Second, read the passages at the head of the questions (if different). Now referring back to the booklet as required, answer all the questions.

3. Write down your answers, as briefly as possible, using only a few words, or at most a couple of sentences each time. As you do so, pray the Lord will show you how your reading and answers are to relate to your own life as a Christian.

4. If you discuss the readings in a group, try to stick to the set themes. It is so easy to go off at tangents, consider many interesting topics, and in the end miss the whole purpose of the study. The questions are to help you avoid doing that, by keeping your thoughts directed to the important, central issues.

5. If you use the recorded teaching that goes with this booklet, listen to it straight through in one sitting before you start your study; then perhaps listen to it again at the conclusion of your study.

6. In a group, do not hurry the study. Its purpose is to help you grow spiritually as well as in understanding, and that takes prayer as well as reading.

FOLLOWING THE LAMB
...wherever He goes

Week One

1. **Mark 10.32**
   What's going on in this scene? Where would you be in this group? How would you be feeling?

2. **Matthew 8.18-27**
   How does the storm on the lake relate to the preceding passage about following Jesus?

   Have you ever followed Jesus into a storm? What happened?

FOLLOWING THE LAMB
...wherever He goes

What does it mean to you to 'follow Jesus'?

3. **Mark 1.9-13**
Where does his Father lead his son?

How is this an expression of his Father's love for him?

FOLLOWING THE LAMB
...wherever He goes

Week Two

4. **Luke 4.24-30; Matthew 2.13-16; Exodus 1.22-2.10; Acts 12 5-10; Exodus 14.15-28**
   What does it mean that God 'watches over your every step'? What steps does he protect?

   What did these men have in common? Why did God rescue them?

   When have you been conscious of God watching over your life?

FOLLOWING THE LAMB
...wherever He goes

5. **Exodus 15.1-21; Revelation 5.1-14**
What did Moses and Miriam sing? Why?

What did the living creatures and elders sing? Why?

When do you sing? Why?

FOLLOWING THE LAMB
...wherever He goes

WEEK THREE

6. **Mark 8.22-33; Matthew 16.13-17**
   This passage is about physical and spiritual blindness. How does Mark 8.27-30 mirror 8.22-26?

It's about knowing and accepting for yourself not just about what others think. — Sometimes it takes a few "nudges" from the Holy Spirit... 2 stages...

Compare with Matthew's version of Peter's confession. Where did Peter get his insight from?

He had a "light bulb" moment. The Holy Spirit Revelation. Direct from God. Divine Revelation.

How could Peter one moment speak such wisdom and the next moment things of Satan? Can you do the same?

He was in his "Human" understanding. Thinking of Himself and being led by his feelings. He saw only half of the picture.

53

FOLLOWING THE LAMB
...wherever He goes

7. Mark 8.31-38; Mark 10.35-45
What, according to Jesus, did it mean to follow him? Has anything changed since he spoke those words? — No

To give up our own plans (control) for our lives submission, to lose our self centeredness.
To seek to serve others without seeking fame, power or position.

How did his disciples respond to what he said? Did they understand? When would they?

They did not understand. On seeing Jesus after He rose again
After His death & resurrection.

What did Jesus have to say about personal ambition in the kingdom?

see above.

FOLLOWING THE LAMB
...wherever He goes

[handwritten: 430-450 years before Jesus was born.]

WEEK FOUR

8. Matthew 27.11-26; Nehemiah 6.1-9; Isaiah 35.8-10

   [handwritten: 80's]

   How was Jesus able to remain silent before his accusers?

   [handwritten: Focused — He was "set" on his journey. Silence is more powerful than argument. He wasn't controlled by his emotions or evil. It was through His silence J. was able to accomplish ur salvation. He didn't allow them control over him. He was self controlled.]

   Imagine you're Sanballat: How would you try to distract Nehemiah from his work?

   [handwritten: Undermine his work, trick him to leave his post. He showed great determination and wisdom. They attacked His character.]

55

FOLLOWING THE LAMB
...wherever He goes

Compare Jesus and Pilate in this scene. Which man is focussed? Which is walking the highway of holiness? Explain. *Jesus - - -*

Why did Pilate have him flogged before he handed Him over to be crucified if he knew J was Innocent M 27 v 26. Pilate was more concerned about His position and not a riot from the crowd

Which man is walking wisely? (see also James 1.2-8)

Jesus - He did not waiver in His Purpose.

How wisely do you walk?

FOLLOWING THE LAMB
...wherever He goes

9. **2 Corinthians 2.14-15**
   What does Paul say is the key to taking Jesus wherever we go?

   Thanksgiving ? Remembrance. we have God's promise of His presence & His victory

   Where do the fights and struggles typically take place? *In my head*

WEEK FIVE

10. **Revelation 2.7, 17, 26; 12.10-12**
    What does it mean to be an overcomer?

    To remain faithful until the end loyally serving God

    person who has victory over trials through their faithfulness & perseverance.

    To live in victory, through faith in Christ

FOLLOWING THE LAMB
...wherever He goes

In the second passage in Revelation in what three ways did they overcome? (12.11)

By the Blood of the lamb — Jesus Res[urrection]
The word of their testimony — our Re[demption]
Surrender their lives
(filled by H/S)

How will you overcome? Can the aroma of Christ be released from your life? Can it be increased?

by stepping out in faith to do what God has said to do.
Step out of comfort zone — be obedient
Faith is not feelings — The fruit of the Spirit grows

11. **Revelation 14.1-5**

   Who are they who sang the new song?   ch 7:4
   144,000 from all the tribes of Israel
   The Righteous. The redeemed
   Both Jews + Gentiles
   gods faithful people

FOLLOWING THE LAMB
...wherever He goes

What have you learned through doing this course about what it means to 'follow the Lamb wherever he goes'?

Its not a part time path.
Its 100% commitment. and not in our own strength
Page 43 - - -

att 10:16

THE WAY OF THE SPIRIT

The Way of the Spirit has a series of Bible reading and study programmes, giving a guide to the whole Bible as seen through the activity and experience of the Holy Spirit.

HOME AND FURTHER STUDY COURSES

Various levels of study and training are available, including short Bible Reading courses similar to this one, and the full-length Reading Course that covers the whole Bible in four six-month parts.

Discipleship training and training for Bible teachers includes full-time residential courses, part-time courses with short residential schools, and mentored training that you can take in local groups and seminars.

For more information **email resources@thewayofthespirit.com**, or go to **www.thewayofthespirit.com/training_overview/**